MW01173690

Bipolar:

Art & Addiction

By

Blackbird Singing

"In the forest, there was a crooked tree and a straight tree. Every day,
the straight tree would say to the crooked tree, "Look at me...I'm tall,
and I'm straight, and I'm handsome. Look at you...you're all crooked
and bent over. No one wants to look at you." And they grew up in
that forest together. And then one day the loggers came, and they
saw the crooked tree and the straight tree, and they said, "Just cut
the straight trees and leave the rest." So the loggers turned all the
straight trees into lumber and toothpicks and paper. And the crooked
tree is still there, growing stronger and stranger every day."

— Tom Waits

Dedication

Hemingway, Faulkner, Fitzgerald, Dickens, O'Neill, Woolf, Handel, Ives, Rachmaninoff, Tchaikovsky, Mingus, Charlie "Yardbird" Parker, Lord Byron, Coleridge, Dickinson, Plath, Keats, Gauguin, O'Keefe, Munch, Pollock, and Rothko, among others.

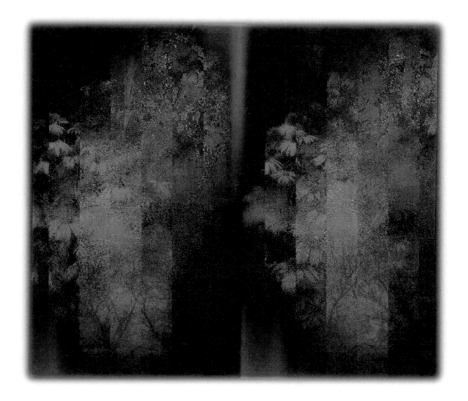

All prisoners & mental patients In all countries

Table of Contents

Prologue

"Fly without wings; Dream with open eyes; See in darkness"

~ Dean Stojanovic

This autobiography is my attempt to create a bridge between the reality that surrounds me and my history, and journey through bipolar illness and art. I hope you will travel with me.

My first sentence was concerned with the difficulties I found write it. I was afraid to be spontaneous, afraid of what I would reveal and what that self-revelation would mean. It was especially difficult for me because I knew that there would be others involved as participants or at least observers in this self-revelation. When I wrote about it as the time, I expressed it as others "witnessing" what happens to me. My use of the word is significant because it shows how I saw the whole situation - as one of judgement. In addition to this fear, I was not used to operating on a spontaneous level. Through the process of my own writing, I grew directed to analyzing situations with myself as the focal point of departure. I was used to operating with "second thoughts," reflectively about where I stood and what was happening.

Robert Schoch of Boston University (Pyramid Quest) agreed after his on-site study of the Great Pyramid that it was like a giant musical instrument. Finally, it is well-known that the sarcophagus in the King's Chamber is tuned to A = 438. Musicians such as Paul Horn have recorded this and made music with it.

"Living is not running from the ghosts

We are unable to fight, but breathing

Affirmations that brutality will never Steel my beauty"

~ post midnight

"Understand me. I am not like an ordinary world. I have my madness, I live in another dimension, and I do not have time for things that have no soul."

Chapter 1

Contemplation On Fragility

I grew up surrounded by love. The kind of love that people are unable to express, that turns inwards and drives you on the brink of madness. The kind of love that only people who were severely unloved could feel. The kind that makes you go chasing ghosts and demons because your life has been so terrifying that these things feel safe in comparison. The kind that affects you in a way that you can only find comfort in chaos, and things like normalcy terrify you.

I grew up with two parents and siblings. That is as normal as it could get, right? We all have our own version of normal. For me, it was hiding under the covers in bed, trying to conjure up beautiful artwork in my mind as I tried to drown out the slurred, screaming voices of my parents coming in from the next room. It is always beautiful in my head.

A flurry of colors, rich, vibrant hues, the brushstrokes twist and twirl, creating beautiful people, beautiful things, and a beautiful life. Everything that I craved for…everything that I ever wanted. I used to reach that place in my mind and find safety and comfort…Before I heard the next bottle smash, bits of wayward glass flew into my room through the doorway.

People say that addicts are trying to fill this deep, dark hole that exists inside their soul that is like a vortex, always consuming, never full. That is why we always crave more…more of everything. More attention, more love, just another drink, another puff, another line, another pill…more, more, more. It is never enough.

The dark hole that exists within the addicted soul is demanding and never satiated. It keeps screaming, 'Fill me up, and we obey. We have no choice. We just want to feel better. We just want to feel full and satisfied… just once, just for a little while.

I should know. Addiction was in my life before I could even understand it. When I was old enough, I went chasing after it because, in a way, it was all I knew. It was an escape from my life and my past and a way for me to still carry it with me. It was my way of myself without having to deal with any of the trauma and pain that I had buried deep within myself. It was fated. Some people inherit wealth or good genes from their families… I inherited generational trauma.

It all started with my grandfather. My paternal grandfather was a sensitive, gentle soul from Cairo, Egypt. It is always the sensitive ones who think that the world is the harshest on them. Maybe it is. For people who lack that particular kind of sensitivity, it is easier for them to get through life unaffected. I envy those people. It must be nice to have that kind of mind-set. My grandfather met his wife, a young Catholic girl in an orphanage in Syria. It must have been quite a meeting because they soon ended up getting married.

My maternal grandmother perfectly complemented my grandfather, and for a while, they were perfectly happy together. She understood his gentle nature. His love of poetry must have wowed her. I wonder if he ever wrote poems for her. He must have. He was a wonderful poet. He could articulate intricate thoughts into words, and reading his poems could make anyone weep. That is a gift only a few artists have. Writers, poets, painters, photographers, musicians, and any other creative thinkers…all of us feel things very intensely.

We have to channel these emotions into our craft, write a story, craft a poem, make a painting, take a picture, or compose a song…and if we do not, we can feel our souls dying bit by bit. I bet my grandfather felt like that, too.

When you are a businessman by day, you do not have much of an outlet for creativity. Nobody makes money writing poetry. My grandfather was a businessman professionally, with the heart and soul of a poet. My grandmother loved that about him. Soon, in search of better opportunities and to provide his family with a better life, my grandfather shifted his family to the French Sector in Shanghai.

It was a great decision. However, eventually when WW2 developed there would be no time for poetry as bullet shells would whizz past their windowsills, barely missing the newly replaced glass pane. Sometimes, they got lucky. Sometimes, they did not, and the window would shatter into a million little pieces.

My grandfather kept a radio in the house so that they could stay abreast of the war. That was a bigger gamble than you could imagine. Keeping a radio was incredibly forbidden at the time. If the Japanese had found out, my grandparents would have been shot on the spot. They were not shot.

My grandfather decided to move his family to Kyoto, Japan, after surviving the war. During the war my father's oldest brother flew in France as a pilot. After the war, my father's youngest brother, moved to England and started a family.

However, sensing that the future would be brighter somewhere else, my grandmother took my dad and moved to the United States. That was the beginning of the end. Some people are not meant to stay alone, I guess.

My grandfather did not take this separation well. He was used to having his loving wife and sons around him. All of a sudden, he found himself alone in Japan. Alone in the house that he once shared with his loved ones.

The halls that must have rung with the laughter and voices of his children were now empty. Loneliness does something to a person, especially if you are a gentle soul. He became really stressed out. He started making mistakes at work, and soon his business was in decline. After one particularly bad business decision and some unbelievably bad luck, all must have seemed lost to him.

His boat had sunk. The boat was the source of his livelihood. He depended on that boat, and when he lost it, he just could not recover, both financially and emotionally. He was bankrupt, and being bankrupt in Japan at that time was a crime, and the punishment was severe.

My grandfather was probably scared out of his mind because he did not know what the Japanese police would do to him if he was arrested and thrown in jail.

Fear, loss, and a constant sense of neglect. It was too much for my grandfather to take. He could not stand to live life in this sorry state. For a man who once had it all, he was lost without everything that made him who he was. His wife and kids are gone, and now his source of income as well. He was on the brink of getting arrested. He decided there was only one thing he could do to fix it.

He had enough money to buy a bottle of alcohol. The good kind if it mattered. It mattered to him. Small details really enhance the scope and tragedy of things. He probably poured one out for the good times and drank the rest for the bad. He turned on a gas stove.

Sylvia Plath wrote in The Bell Jar, "Death must be so beautiful. To lie in the soft brown earth, with the grasses waving above one's head, and listen to silence. To have no yesterday, and no tomorrow. To forget time, to forgive life, to be at peace."

I wonder if my grandfather felt a calmness and peace wash over him as the last signs of life escaped his body. Did he see the light and realize this was an end to all his earthly troubles, or did he die, choking, in pain, and then fall into nothingness?

We would never know.

What I do know is that his death really did a number on my dad. He always wondered why my grandfather would choose death over life, choosing to leave him and his family for an early grave. It became an obsession for him. Only alcohol could quieten the noise.

Photographer and poet Tracy Hamby wanted to leave California and come East to live with me several years ago. But he died in California with his wife by his side.

I ended up in a mental hospital. I kept looking for him & thought he was there. In the mental hospital I thought I saw Christ, Ken Kesey (who wrote "One Flew Over the Cuckoo's Nest"), the pope who was a woman, all the apostles. I did not know who I was. I asked a woman there one night. She said, "you are the god of light." Photography means writing with light: photo-graphy.

When we gathered for meals, Jesus was helping all the patients with their food. I kept waiting for him to give us communion by breaking the rolls they gave us. He did not. I thought I had to and broke bread waiting to give the others communion, but they left to go in to incredibly powerful music and art therapy.

I knew I was an artist from my earliest years and in art therapy, I excelled. But in music therapy I was fearful. But in that mental hospital I found out that I am also a surprisingly good musician.

I could not walk. I kept falling. I was in a wheelchair. During the 4 smoking breaks, other patients and some staff would wheel me into a large fenced in yard. I could smoke! I could breathe! The freedom!

The sunlight! The moon and stars! My heart opened and I had hope and had found fellowship with other mentally ill. This happened to me every time I was involuntarily committed to mental hospitals.

I was committed many times. I have hallucinations.

I always see angels. They surround me and protect me wherever I go. Then and now.

Chapter 2

Vortex Of Energy

My father and grandmother moved to NYC and became US citizens. They lived peacefully in the French sector of Shanghai before that, where my father and his two brothers went to French schools. Their first language was French.

My dad had inherited his father's demons and befriended quite a few of his own. He married my mother; I am sure there was love in their relationship at some point. My American mother was born to a couple in Brooklyn, NY. She was a legendary beauty. She got thyroid cancer when she was 18. The surgery was botched which resulted in a lump near in her neck, but my dad still loved her and married her. My mother had 3 brothers and 1 sister (who died as a child of influenza). My mother's oldest brother was my favorite relative. Unlike the rest of my family, he understood me. He did not believe that there was a god, he was an atheist.

I would like to believe my sister and I were born out of love. However, love is not enough when your very soul is troubled. My dad would drink, and my mom would smoke like a chimney, and they would fight and fight and fight some more until the sun came up, the first breath of morning light reflected in the Hudson River, and I would wonder what it looked like from my little bedroom in our apartment.

I remember I would stand in the doorway to my bedroom, half obscured by the dim lights of the hallway, and listen to them argue and fight day in and day out.

They fought because they cared about each other. That is what I made myself believe. They must care about each other deeply to get so worked up like this. Why else would they bother? It was a nice thought, but even as a child, I knew it was not an honest one. My dad would get drunk and cheat on my mom. She would cry and scream at him and throw things, but she still stayed with him. He would apologize and grovel, and she would take him back if he promised never to do it again. He always did it again.

My father had flaws, sure. Everybody does. But I loved him. I loved him deeply, and I was by his side on the day that he died at the age of 91 in, Florida. He was worried, fretting about whether he would be forgiven for being unfaithful to my mother.

I offered whatever reassurance I could, but I knew it was not the reassurance that he wanted. He could not have gotten my mother's absolution, though; she had died at the age of 75 from heart disease. Sometimes, realization comes when every other ship has sailed. I was sorry to think that it happened to my dad.

I knew he was about to go. He had always been such a presence. His drinking did not define him. We did. The good times we spent together did. He would put my sister and me to sleep every night in our twin beds, singing, "Goodnight, my love, the tired old moon is descending".

I can still hear his song in my head sometimes. I squeezed his hand and asked him to tell me if there was life after death when he died…and I was blown away when he found a way to do it.

When he died, my father's second wife had given the funeral director a watch for him to wear. It was an old watch, and it did not work anymore. The funeral home had put the watch on him when they dressed him and placed him in his casket. When I approached the casket to say my final goodbye, I was astonished to notice that it showed the right time. I ran to the funeral director to ask him whether they fixed the watch. They said no.

I knew right then that this was my father's doing. It was a miracle. My dad was telling me that there was a life after death. My dad was an ordinary man with extraordinary gifts. It should not have surprised me that he managed to pull this off. He lived and worked in 8 different countries and had travelled six months away from our family every year. He had many affairs overseas and had two children outside the country. It did not bother me.

I felt the grief of my father's passing, but weirdly, I knew that he was watching over me, and everything would be okay. That night, I dreamt I was flying around my bedroom like a bird. That was a sign that better days were still ahead of us. That was then. I am choosing to tell my story now. It might not always be linear because that is not how my mind works. I have been in and out of mental institutions all my life. That is what happens when you are a bipolar drug addict with the soul of an artist.

Mental hospitals, they say, are where you find angels and saints. Those who diagnosed – schizophrenic, psychotic, bipolar … names that, to some, carry the weight of stigma, but to me, they are a part of who I am. A Bipolar Artist who sees angels and saints. Guardians sent by the archangel Michael himself.

It always comes down to this very moment. The gentle melodies of "Playing for Change" fill the air, a harmonious chorus from musicians around the world, singing for peace and an end to war and poverty. I support them, and I listen, searching for peace.

Here in my garden, I sit with my loyal companion, Lambchop. She's not just a dog; she's my guardian angel, too. Her ears, resembling angelic wings, caught my eye in a picture online. I transformed that image into a tintype, a precious keepsake. She sits beside me now in this haven I have created … my sanctuary within a fence. Over time, I have had three guardian angels – Harpo, McPherson, and now, Lambchop.

The music of the world and the song of the birds surround me. Birds, the holy spirits on Earth, share their songs with one another, and we humans are privileged to hear. Birds often visit my garden, which is adorned with morning glories, vibrant vines, and perennial blooms.

Saint Francis and the Buddha stand side by side, statues that watch over this sacred place. Solar lights and lanterns illuminate the garden at night under the gaze of our moon. I yearn for visitors in the daylight, yearn for visitors when I am well. You see, I am bipolar, and when the darkness descends, I find myself in the stark world of mental hospitals. Electroconvulsive therapy, or ECT, is a shock to my system, a desperate attempt to dispel the shadows. But amidst it all, I got addicted to propofol, the same drug that claimed Michael Jackson's life.

Bipolar: a constant dance between light and shadow. I find solace in the teachings of Buddhism, where the search for peace and serenity intertwines with spiritual principles. Enlightenment is a beacon, not limited to Buddha or Jesus, but within reach for all of us. "The message of the Buddha," I contemplate, "Pain, old age, and death are not to be feared. Acceptance and living in the nano moment are keys."

Looking up to the heavens and stars in the vast sky, I am reminded of our insignificance in the grand cosmos. We are stardust, part of the universe's intricate system, deserving of our place. No need for validation or explanations. Life itself is the greatest gift.

I do not seek mere happiness or fleeting contentment. Emotions come and go like waves in the ocean. My quest is serenity, peace of mind, and being true to myself. It demands focus amidst the chaos, warding off the distractions of others' delusions and misconceptions. Control, an illusion, only over myself do I have a semblance of power.

Time is that elusive concept, both a marker and a constraint in the physical realm. My journey in 2022 is to embrace the present, to confront the material world without forsaking my soul, and to prepare for the inevitable end. A gift acknowledged, a life to honor. Balance, the elusive center of spiritual sobriety, is a constant battle for physical, mental, and emotional equilibrium.

The path to integration is to be whole. "I look for an easy answer, a quick fix, a free lunch," I confess. "But the reality of existence beckons." In the grand scheme of life, I am but a grain of sand sculpted by the sands of time. A thirst for enlightenment, for meaning beyond the mundane, keeps me striving. And in my dream, the boundaries blur. A room filled with art, with a house adorned in sparkles – a house I could not leave. Lambchop and my sister enter, and I awaken, holding on to the magic of the dream.

Time, that elusive notion, remains a mystery to me. I have been a wanderer, disregarding the constraints of days, weeks, and months. But in 2022, I confront the reality of time and existence, and with each day, I become more grounded in the now. The quest for spiritual sobriety continues, a constant balancing act. I respect my limitations, avoid the allure of grandiosity, and acknowledge that all life is special, including mine.

Meetings, the cornerstone of my life: I get up, I show up, I pay attention. The program has taught me to wear life-like, loose-fitting clothing to not take myself too seriously. My goal is to keep moving in that direction. I think back to Saturday night movies at the club meetings with friends –. Good meetings, good movies, good times.

Meeting makers make it, they say. The program has ingrained in me the importance of balance and not taking life too seriously. In the end, it is about giving yourself grace. Interacting with the world and oneself with goodwill and kindness. It is a practice, like yoga or running, and an ongoing journey. As I sit in my garden, surrounded by the serenity I have cultivated, I find solace in the simplicity of the present moment.

The birds sing, the solar lights glow, and Lambchop, my guardian angel, rests by my side. In the dance of light and shadow, I seek my own balance, my own serenity, and the beauty of living in the now.

Chapter 3

Nourishment

Did you know that religious people are susceptible to drug addiction? Yes, it sounds surprising, doesn't it? You would think that someone who is deeply religious and has a close relationship with God would be able to fend off the depravity of addiction and resist the allure of drugs, the one weapon that doom souls to hell for all eternity. Drugs chip away at the humanity in you, bit by bit. They eat away at your soul, languidly nibbling away at your conscience, corroding your moral compass, and burning away any sense of decency and grace that you once might have possessed.

A lot of people think you can just quit using drugs. You do not get done with drugs. They get done with you. Once they do, you are left in shambles, a shell of the person that you used to be, shivering, afraid, and too ashamed to look into the mirror to see the ghosts of the atrocities you committed staring back at you.

So, why are religious people so susceptible to addiction? Religion is a type of addiction, really. It requires blind faith and utter devotion, and that is what an addict has towards their drug of choice. Karl Marx once said, 'Religion is the opiate of the masses.' It ensnares you, bewitches you, makes you do things you never thought you would do. The kind of myopic vision that you develop, whether you are looking through the lens of religion or you are on heroin, you are both fixated on the same thing. Feel the warmth.

Feel the light. Feel like you belong somewhere- it is not that different, really.

The transition came easily to me as well. My faith in God was strong, and I believed that if I just prayed hard enough, God would one day fix all my problems. He will make my parents stop drinking and fighting, and we will have a normal, happy family once again. I would spend hours reading the Bible and going to church. I just needed to prove myself. One more prayer, just one more hit. It is not that different. I would always believe that my next prayer would be granted. I always thought that the next fix would get me to that coveted state of bliss, but it never did- but I am getting ahead of myself. I was deeply religious growing up, taking solace in God when I did not have many other sources of comfort in my life.

People turn to religion because they need to find meaning in something greater than themselves. I desperately needed to believe that growing up. I needed to believe that there was something greater than this world and our existence. The thought of us being here, on earth, just existing, going through the motions of life, and then dying without any higher purpose was terrifying. I did not even want to consider that possibility. So, religion helped me. In fact, I even wanted to be a nun. Denounce a life of worldly pleasure and become a bride of Jesus Christ to live a humble life devoted to quiet contemplation and worship of God.

My desire for a lifetime of nunnery lasted till I was sixteen. I do not know if you can understand this feeling if you have not experienced something similar, but I will try to explain it to you the best that I can. I grew up Catholic, and I found the beauty in my religion. The art, the stories, and the sense of belonging that I experienced always made me feel safe when my world was full of chaos. I would just sit in the church pew as the altar candles shimmered against the stained-glass window pains and breathe in the heady smell of incense that filled up the room.

The choir would sing, and their voices would sound angelic, bringing me the comfort that I always craved. Most of all, I cherished my connection to God. I relished the idea that there was an all-powerful figure always watching over me, who was always there for me no matter what. I did not have a lot of people like that in my life, so God made a good substitute.

I remember playing in the playgrounds at my grammar's school church and getting grass stains on my Sunday best. I loved my pure white communion dress and stockings. I always thought my lamb was a soft and gentle one. I grew up with these fantastical, divine thoughts and images in my mind, and I always thought I would become a part of the church one day. Join a convent and take up my vocation as a nun.

I believed I was here to answer a higher calling, and the best way to do that was by becoming a nun.

However, when I turned 16, I shared my desire with a nun. She told me something that quite surprised me because I did not expect that advice from her. She told me to challenge my faith before devoting my entire life to it.

This was a new concept for me. Usually, the only thing people had ever told me was to have blind faith and to question faith is the highest sin of blasphemy and pride. However, I was growing up at that time, and the nun's advice made sense. Why shouldn't I test myself before making a lifetime commitment and giving up every worldly pleasure? I should not make this decision lightly. So, I started testing my faith. I started exploring different facets of the outside world that I had previously closed myself off to. I was on a journey of self-discovery, and I would not commit to nunnery until and unless I was one hundred percent sure that I was on the right path.

I thought this journey would end up fortifying my faith. I ended up losing it entirely. See, religion is like a house of cards. The foundation of belief is always shaky because it requires an insurmountable amount of trust and blind faith. You are asked to believe in an invisible man in the sky who created the world, who is always watching you and judging you, so you better not step out of line. Many people blindly believe that. That blind belief is essential because the moment you start asking questions, the shaky foundation crumbles, and the house of cards come tumbling down.

I lost my religion once I read Thomas Aquinas and St. Augustine. Their philosophies blew my mind wide open. Aquinas said, 'God can be proved by natural reason,' and even though this went against the tenets of Catholicism, it made a world of sense to me. According to Augustine, the earth was brought into existence ex nihilo by a perfectly good and just God, who created man. The earth is not eternal; the earth, as well as time, has both a beginning and an end. What struck me about his work was the fact that he said, 'Man, on the other hand, was brought into existence to endure eternally'.

That hit me hard. Endure eternally. That meant that I had to deal with all the pain and that I had learned were a part of life, forever, without any escape. If it was our lot in life to 'endure', why should I suffer this fate, denying myself everything good that the world has to offer? No way. I was done being the good little girl. I had always strived so hard to be. Now, I was going to do whatever I wanted to do, so help me God.

All these realizations in my life were happening simultaneously with other things that I took in my stride as a part of growing up. I never thought that I would ever drink or turn to substances because of how alcohol messed up my parents, but I would be lying if I said that I did not have a morbid curiosity towards them. After all, if drugs and alcohol are so potent that they can make you forget how to care for your own family, surely there must be something amazing about them. Something so great that you would choose the substance and the drinks over your own daughters.

Looking back, I must admit that I was naive, thinking that I could somehow get away from all of it unscathed. A childhood like mine leaves deep scars that manifest in different ways throughout your lifetime. These scars do not heal; they flare up angry and red and demand your attention until you do something to placate them. You find yourself looking for new ways to placate them and the voices screaming in your head. Anything for silence.

I was sixteen the first time I tried an opiate. I got hurt and was taken to the emergency room. The doctor decided that the pain was too intense for me to cope with on my own, so he prescribed a little pill called Percocet to me. At home, when it was time to take my medicine, I took it out of its plastic, orange trappings and put one pill in the palm of my hand. It is so small and round, like a little button. This little pill is supposed to take all my pain away? I popped open the pill and chased it down with some water. What happened next blew my mind.

A beautiful warmth slowly crept its way up my body. It started making its way up from my fingertips and coursed its way throughout my body. I felt like somebody had wrapped me up in a huge blanket made of the softest and fuzziest fleece you could imagine. I felt like I was bathed in a golden glow that went down my throat and illuminated me from within. I felt as though God himself had cradled me up in his arms and carried me to heaven. I was in absolute heaven. I had never felt this way before, and suddenly, nothing hurt anymore.

There was no more pain, no more bad feelings. Best of all, for the first time in my life, there was quiet. That voice in my mind was always screaming at me, always telling me that I was not good enough, that I would not amount to anything shut down. It seemed as if the Percocet had gagged that bitch. I smiled slowly and blinked my eyes, trying to understand what was happening to me.

This feeling was so pure and beautiful, and suddenly, I felt terrified that I would never feel this way again. I had to feel this way again. It was the first time I had felt good in years. Good, and not just the pretend good you try to convince everybody that you are. I felt warm, safe, and loved. At that moment, I knew that I did not need anyone else. I had started to identify as agnostic, but on Percocet, I was sure that God was real, and I was wrapped up in his blanket at that moment.

I lay down and felt the soft sheets touching my skin. The simple cotton and polyester blend sheets felt like they were made from pure Egyptian cotton with a ten thousand thread count. My eyelids felt heavy, so I closed my eyes, just letting the warmth and the bliss take over. This was what I wanted to feel all that time when I was searching for a connection, searching for a link to God. All I needed was this little white pill.

It scared me how intense my reaction was to this pill, but that fear was not enough to deter me from trying to chase that feeling again. I knew that I had to feel this way again. If I did not, life would not be worth living. That should have been a sign. A sign that I was already falling through the hole. Only an addict would think this way, but I did not realize that. Nobody becomes an addict on purpose.

I did not know that this one moment would define how I lived the rest of my life, but we never know in the beginning, do we? I threw caution to the winds and started chasing the highs. It would change my life in ways that I never knew possible. When I look back at my life from the present to that moment, I wonder how I managed to cope with it all. I was a teenager who was just looking to find some meaning in life. I found solace in drugs but did not really understand my purpose.

Eventually, I figured out how to embrace the universe within. My mind was unique. It was my greatest asset and my biggest weakness. I exist in a constant state of duality. "Do not feel lonely. The entire universe is inside you," I would often whisper to myself during those dark and turbulent nights when my bipolar disorder threatened to consume me. Those words, a soothing mantra, reminded me that I was never truly alone in my struggles. The cosmos, with its infinite mysteries and wonders, existed within me, offering comfort and strength.

As I journeyed through life, I came to understand that love was not an external destination but an intrinsic part of my being. "Lovers do not finally meet somewhere. They are in each other all along," I mused. My romantic escapades, like brushstrokes on a canvas, were expressions of the love that dwelled within me, waiting to be shared with kindred souls.

During moments of despair, I found comfort in the wisdom of Rumi. "There are a thousand ways to kneel and kiss the ground; there are a thousand ways to go home again." In those depths of despair, I discovered countless paths to inner peace and redemption, each a unique journey back to the sanctuary of my own soul. Amidst the storms that raged within, I remembered the power of these words. "Raise your words, not your voice. It is rain that grows flowers, not thunder."

I learned to channel my emotions into my art and my words, allowing them to bloom like vibrant blossoms amidst the chaos. Life often felt like a dream, a surreal and ephemeral existence. "This place is a dream. Only a sleeper considers it real. Then death comes like dawn, and you wake up laughing at what you thought was your grief." The difficulties of my addictions were like the fleeting scenes of a dream, teaching me not to take them too seriously.

To navigate the labyrinth of love, I followed the guidance of Rumi once more. "Would you become a pilgrim on the road of love? The first condition is that you make yourself humble as dust and ashes." Humility became my compass, guiding me through the tumultuous seas of passion and desire.

In my darkest moments, I recited these words like a mantra: "You are not a drop in the ocean. You are the entire ocean in a drop."

I constantly needed to remind myself that my existence held immeasurable depth and significance, even when it felt like I was drowning in the vastness of my emotions. The world often tried to confine me, to limit my potential, but I refused to yield. "If the foot of the trees were not tied to the earth, they would be pursuing me. For I have blossomed so much, I am the envy of the gardens."

I allowed my creative spirit to flourish without restraint, becoming a source of inspiration, determined to let my work speak for me. As I confronted the vastness of the universe within me, I embraced my role in its cosmic dance. "Stop acting so small. You are the universe in ecstatic motion." These words reminded me that I was an integral part of the grand symphony of existence, my emotions and experiences harmonizing with the entire galaxy itself.

In my journey of self-discovery, I heeded the call to create my own myth. "Do not be satisfied with stories, how things have gone with others. Unfold your myth." My bipolar disorder and addiction were not a curse. This was my cross to bear in life, and it would only make me stronger with each passing day that I refused to succumb to it.

Through the trials and tribulations of my journey, dealing with abuse, bipolar disorder and addiction, I learned that the universe was not merely around me; it was within me. Within that universe, I found the strength to embrace my true self, an artist in perpetual motion, painting the canvas of my existence with vibrant hues of passion and creativity.

Chapter 4

Transcendental Origins

I remember the days when faith was my anchor, the guiding light through the tumultuous waters of life. There was a time when I saw the world through the stained glass of Catholicism. The church bells would toll, and I would eagerly make my way to the pew, my heart filled with devotion. God was my confidant, my refuge, the silent listener to my anguished prayers.

Growing up, my faith was a sanctuary in a household marred by shadows of neglect and misunderstanding. It was there, in the dimly lit church, that I found solace from the turbulence of my mind.

Do you know what it is like to believe in something so fervently you refuse to see sense? You refuse to accept any rationale, take any evidence presented against your beliefs as a personal attack, and decide that you will stick with what you believe no matter what.

In order to be truly religious, we have to adopt this type of head-in-the-sand approach towards life. Blindly obeying the rules and laws that your religion imposes, condemn others who do not, and walk around with a holier-than-thou air and a smug look of religious superiority. I am not saying everyone who has faith is like this. It's actually far from it.

True believers are people are spiritual and do not feel the need to flaunt their faith or wear it on their sleeve; they simply walk with the light of God in their heart. They have a close, personal relationship with their faith, so they do not feel the need to declare it to every single person that they meet. Religion should be an immensely profound yet deeply personal experience.

Maybe it is my bipolar mind or a natural, innate sense of curiosity, but it is hard for me to accept things just because someone said so. I have always had questions; I just didn't't know it was okay to ask them. As soon as I realized that I could, I started poking holes in my own beliefs.

Beliefs do not do well when you start poking holes in them. As bits of knowledge start permeating through, more of your old ideals slip away. At least, that is what happened to me. For a while, I was not even sure if God really existed. Now, I know that He does, and for that, I will be eternally grateful.

People say that God only gives us as much suffering as we can handle. That is a bad-up way of thinking. Why would God, who is supposed to be the creator of everything in the universe and the very embodiment of love and forgiveness, create specific forms of torture just to mess with us? No, I think suffering is a purely human achievement. We are the ones that create pain and suffering in the world. We love hurting other people. Some people get off on it. Some of us are just hurting, so we lash out and hurt others, while others are the object of people's hurt.

God gave us free will. Was that His way of letting us find our own paths to redemption or create a greater opportunity to destroy ourselves? I shall never know. Nothing good has ever come out of giving humans free rein to do something. We tend to develop megalomaniac tendencies; we delude ourselves into believing we are the Gods because we are given the ability to build stuff and give birth to other humans.

I grew firmly agnostic after reading the philosophies of St. Augustine and Thomas Aquinas. That much is true, but for some reason, some part of God remained in my heart, and I have always been interested in exploring spirituality.

I think somewhere down the line, life found a way to unravel even my most devout convictions. The whispers of doubt began to creep into my heart as I grappled with the intensity of my emotions and the stark reality that something just did not feel right about certain religious rules and values that were forced upon me. I had always appreciated the straightforward nature of religion. Do this, do not do that. It took away the burden of making decisions about life and made things seem simple. If only I was a simple girl. But that inner rebelliousness eventually came out, through drugs, through reckless behavior.

Being bipolar means you are no stranger to wild changes in your approach to life. I was used to it. The mood swings, the darkness that descended upon me like a suffocating shroud—it all seemed so contrary to the teachings of my faith. This is not what I signed up for. I was looking for comfort and acceptance when all I found were more restrictions without any answers.

I started to explore alternative philosophies, seeking answers to the unrelenting questions that gnawed at my soul. I allowed opiates to ensnare my senses, falling deeper and deeper into their trap as they helped me feel every sensation that I was searching for in religion and other things. The light of God, a mother's love, a father's support- once I got high on Percocet, it felt like I never missed any of these things at all.

My Catholic upbringing felt like a distant memory, replaced by a desire to understand the world through a different lens. I read about Buddhism, dabbled in New Age spirituality, and delved into the teachings of philosophers who questioned the very essence of existence. It was a desperate search for meaning, a way to make sense of the chaos that raged within my mind.

As I delved deeper into this spiritual exploration, I felt the tethers of my faith slowly loosen. The rituals that had once brought me solace now felt hollow, the church's doctrines distant and detached from the tumultuous reality of my life. I yearned for something tangible, something that could bridge the chasm between my creativity and my suffering.

Percocet had come into my life like a siren's call. It promised relief from the relentless turmoil that bipolar disorder inflicted upon me. The pills provided a fleeting escape, a respite from the never-ending noise that buzzed like static on the TV inside my brain. It was never quiet inside my head, but opiates made me feel nice and numb. I could never feel so mellow without them.

As the warmth and numbness spread languidly through my bloodstream, I grew used to feeling a strange detachment from the world, from my own identity. I was used to feeling like for most of my life. That feeling faded away into the shadows whenever I got high. I was at peace. It calmed the raging fire inside my mind, lulling me into a deceptive sense of peace.

There is a saying that 'heroin gives you bliss but takes away everything else you have, even your life'.. Well, that is the truth and can be said for all opiates. Percocet is one hell of a gateway drug. Once I got high off Percocet, I wanted to see what different drugs would do to my mind. I love living when I do not want to die. Life has so many different feelings that one can experience, and there is no better way to experience a wider range of emotions and sensations than to experiment with different drugs.

That is how I viewed my habits as a creative exploration of the mind and with the help of mind-altering substances that would help me experience every sensation I could imagine and some even beyond my imagination. I was neck-deep in my love affair with opiates. It was time to bring some new drugs to the party.

The drug culture was different back in the 70s. While the so-called 'normal 'people were super uptight, the hippies, the creative souls who just wanted to live a life of peace and love, were more accepting. They were my people. I believe angels walk amongst us on earth, and I see them all the time. I see angels in the faces of my friends. I see them smiling at me through different dogs, cats, and rabbits, along with other animals. Angels are among us, and for some reason, they make themselves very visible to me. This is why I have not fully given up on God yet. Angels give me hope that God is still there, somewhere.

Back in the 70s, weed culture was becoming more prevalent, especially among the flower children. You could always find someone smoking a joint on the street, and hey, weed smokers are the nicest people you would ever meet. All you have to do is ask them if they have a joint, and they will happily let you have a few drags off their jay. I started keeping my own stash soon. Weed is fun. It made me feel hungry, which was important to me as opiates killed my appetite.

I was able to eat and enjoy food. It made me laugh. It allowed me to deal with life without taking myself too seriously. What is most important is that it felt great. My head would be buzzing, and I would be sitting in the garden, feeling the grass underneath my feet as the air around me started going fuzzy.

I also started doing Quaaludes. If you are a part of the younger generation, you would probably be thinking, 'What are Quaaludes?' They have been mostly wiped out of existence now by the government. However, back then, Quaaludes were the party drug of the decade. In fact, people loved 'ludes so much that you would find juice bars and discos selling them with alcohol.

I still remember the first time I took Quaaludes. The room seemed to blur and warp, colors blending into surreal patterns that danced before my eyes. Reality itself became a distant echo, a dreamlike landscape where the boundaries of time and space dissolved into a mesmerizing haze. It was as if I had stepped into a different dimension, one where nothing else mattered except the absolute joy I was experiencing, as if reality never even existed. I did not have to worry about school or my parents fighting. All I had to do was chill out and enjoy the ride.

Hanging out with the party crowd, you are bound to encounter someone who has got cocaine. I would see my friends lay gigantic lines of coke on glass tables that we would snort with metal straws. My jaw would clench, and my pupils became like pinpricks. With eyes as wide as saucers, I would feel the music vibrating to the rhythm of my heartbeat. I did drugs to feel. You feel everything on cocaine, and you feel nothing at all. It is the best of both worlds, and for someone like me, I lived for the rush.

During this time, I also began drinking copious amounts of alcohol. I would down White Russians as if I were drinking water. I was no stranger to alcohol. Alcohol was to me what milk probably was to other children. Other kids might trip over their milk bottles lying on the floor next to their beds, but I would be falling over the empty vodka bottles left behind by my father. I grew to associate the strong smell of whiskey with my father's arrival. I would often see my mother with a bottle of wine in her hand. To me, alcohol was no big deal.

It did what I wanted it to do. It was an escape. It took me away from my reality, my purposeless existence, and the small-minded banality of the people around me. I hate feeling trapped. I was not able to physically escape and get as far away as I could from my world, but I could escape it in my mind. I did not have to care.

The screaming in my head would die down for a few hours, and I would pretend I was someone else, someone glamorous and cool, someone far away from this hell. Drugs and faith may have been the same side of each coin ideologically,.

I learned that, to my dismay, eventually.

Chapter 5

Religious Energy

My journey as an artist has been an intricate dance between my life and my art, a perpetual fusion of experiences and expressions that shape the canvas of my existence. I often wonder about my purpose here on earth. Why am I here? Who am I supposed to be? To simplify things, I tell myself that I am Blackbird. I am a photographer and a painter, but I am more than just a creator of images and colors. I am a vessel for emotions, a conduit for life's profound experiences that manifest as art.

I am bipolar, but I choose to think of that as a strength rather than a drawback. It makes my life difficult. It makes my mind work differently from other people. But different is good. Different is unique. For me, art has never been a mere hobby or a career choice; it is a way of breathing, a way of existing. I have always known that my art is not just a reflection of my life but a testament to the depth of my experiences. Whether I am capturing a fleeting moment with my camera, splashing colors onto a canvas, or looking at musical notes dance around me as I listen to music, my work is a product of the life I lead.

I have been told that I am a consummate artist, and it is a description that both humbles and motivates me. I have spent countless hours immersed in the world of photography, seeking the perfect shot that encapsulates the essence of a scene, person, or emotion. I have explored the vast spectrum of emotions, from joy to heartache, and I have channeled them through my lens, translating feelings into images that tell stories of their own.

My photography is not just about capturing smiles and beautiful landscapes; it is about evoking emotions and inviting viewers to share in the moment. I remember one photograph, taken during a rain-soaked evening in the heart of the city. The glistening streets reflected the neon lights, and I looked around, thinking, this is what New York is supposed to look like. I saw the regular dregs of the city, discarded and neglected people spending time together on the sidewalk.

One day, a man under a tattered umbrella caught my gaze. His eyes, though weathered by hardship, sparkled with a flicker of hope. In that instant, I saw resilience, the human spirit enduring in the face of adversity. The resulting photograph spoke volumes, and it is one of my proudest creations, a testament to the emotions I have witnessed and felt in my journey.

My paintings are another side of my artistic expression, a realm where I let colors and strokes flow freely, much like my emotions. I have never been one to meticulously plan my paintings; instead, I let my feelings guide me. When I am engulfed in sorrow, I find solace in the blues and grays on my palette. When joy dances through my veins, vibrant and bold hues emerge. My paintings are a mirror to my soul, and each brushstroke is an echo of my heart.

I often find myself using music to amplify the intensity of my emotions. Listening to haunting vocals or a passionate guitar riff is a cathartic experience, a channel through which I can translate the complex rhythms of life into melodies that resonate with the soul. The music I listen to reflects my journey in life, a sonic documentation of my experiences, and a reflection of my evolving self.

My writing is yet another way of brushing my life onto a canvas. It is a medium that allows me to introspect and dissect the labyrinth of my thoughts and emotions. Through words, I can construct worlds, breathe life into characters, and create intricate narratives that take me away from the harsh reality of the world. When I write, I do not have to be Blackbird. I can be anyone else. I feel God-like, creating worlds that have no limits and characters that are brave enough to do things I always wanted to do. Every sentence I craft is a revelation of my inner self, a window into the passions and demons that fuel my artistic endeavors.

What sets me apart as an artist is my unrelenting pursuit of new experiences. I believe that life is an unending source of inspiration, and I have made it a point to embrace every opportunity that allows me to transform experiences into art. My relationship with drugs is no secret to you by now. When drugs still captivated me, I was obsessed with how each substance altered my mind and how I could use that state of mind to create my art.

On LSD, the world was full of colors and patterns, brighter, more mysterious, and mystical than what my sober mind could ever dream up. An LSD trip can truly take you on an enlightening journey within yourself to experience death. Not death in the way that we think, as in the ending of a life, but the death of your ego.

When you experience ego-death, you can see all the ways you have harmed yourself and the people around you. If you want, you can use it as an opportunity to start over. I would paint in bright purple, pink, and green. I would take pictures of myself and see a wide-eyed woman in the mirror, marveling at the cataclysmic changes going on in her mind.

Quaaludes would help slow down the world around me. My brush strokes would be languid, luxurious, and free. The images would melt into each other, like Salvador Dali's melting clocks, but for me, anything I painted would converge into each other. I would find the beauty in everything around me on Percocet. The sky would look bright, and the air would feel extra crisp when I woke up in the morning. I would try to capture how I felt on film.

Creating art on cocaine was a trip on its own. Finding the focus to create was the first obstacle, but when I did, my art would feel like it was ready to jump off the page. With dynamic images, thick outlines, and a crowded canvas, I could not get every idea on the page fast enough. I would be creating at a hundred miles per hour. The results were interesting, to say the least.

In the heart of it all, I realized that my art was not just about capturing beauty or experimenting with drugs; it was about capturing truth... The everyday moments, the mundane routines, and the quiet introspection are equally significant. A simple cup of coffee in the morning can spark an idea for a painting. The way sunlight filters through the leaves can inspire a photograph. The cadence of a conversation can inspire lyrics for a song.

When I faced personal struggles, art became my refuge. During a period of heartbreak, my paintings were an outlet for my pain and confusion. Each canvas became a place to release my sorrow, and the act of creation itself was a form of healing. The strokes of color on the canvas mirrored the emotional turbulence within me, and as I painted, I found a measure of catharsis.

On the other side, the euphoria of success and joyous milestones in my life found expression through vivid and celebratory artwork. My photographs documented the smiles, my paintings overflowed with vibrant colors, and my music resonated with pure happiness. While the connection between my life and art is profound, it is not always easy. There are times when I struggle to convey the depths of my experiences when words, colors, or notes fall short of encapsulating the full spectrum of my emotions. Yet, it is in these moments of challenge that I find growth and evolution as an artist.

Art is not just a medium of expression; it is a conversation. It is a dialogue between the creator and the audience, a silent exchange of emotions and thoughts. I have come to appreciate the fact that every individual who views my work interprets it through the lens of their own experiences. My art becomes a mirror for their emotions, and in that exchange, a connection is forged, a shared moment of understanding.

Living with bipolar disorder has been a complex and often turbulent journey. The emotional highs and lows have painted the backdrop of my life, influencing my art in profound ways. However, there was a period when I sought solace and inspiration through substances, believing they could enhance my artistic vision. I experimented with various drugs, hoping to see the world in new and vibrant ways. For a while, it seemed like these substances were opening doors to unexplored realms. of creativity. When I used opiates, the world became a serene and dreamlike landscape, and my paintings took on a serene, almost surreal quality. Cocaine brought bursts of frenetic energy, which I thought imbued my work with intensity. When I experimented with LSD, the boundaries of reality blurred, and I created abstract and psychedelic art that seemed to tap into the cosmos.

Alcohol, too, played its part in altering my perception and creative process. I believed that it liberated my inhibitions, allowing me to express emotions more freely. As my substance of choice changed, so did the subject matter of my art. I thought I was seeing the world through new and exciting lenses, creating art that was daring and innovative.

Yet, the truth was that these substances took more than they gave. They affected not only my mental and physical health but also the authenticity of my work. The intense highs were inevitably followed by crushing lows, and my creative process became erratic and unreliable. My art lacked the depth and coherence that I once had, reflecting the chaos within me.

But life has a way of offering moments of clarity, even in the darkest of times. It was during one of these moments that I realized I had been using substances to escape from the very emotions I should have been channeling into my art. I recognized that the vibrant colors I sought in the world could be found within the canvas, waiting to be painted with every emotion, every experience, and every connection that shaped me.

When I eventually sobered up, I was determined to prove to myself that I did not need substances to be a good artist. In the process, I discovered that the raw, unfiltered emotions I experienced were powerful enough to drive my creative process without the need for external stimulants.

My artwork underwent a transformation after getting sober. The clarity of sobriety allowed me to channel my bipolar experiences more authentically and effectively. My paintings became a reflection of the full spectrum of my emotions, from the depths of despair to the heights of euphoria. The photographs I took were infused with a newfound sense of focus and purpose, capturing the intricate beauty of being present, of being aware, and of being awake in the NOW.

As I created art in sobriety, I noticed the vivid colors in the air more keenly, not because of substances but as a product of deep immersion in the creative process. The emotions I perceived as hues, abstract shapes, and colors continued to find expression in my work, revealing a new depth and intensity.

The theme of angels walking among us remains a central element in my art. These "angels" were not the result of substances but rather a reflection of my belief in the goodness and love that can be found in the people around us. The clarity of sobriety allowed me to express this concept more authentically, creating artwork that resonated with both my emotions and the emotions of those who viewed it. Sobriety has been my most profound and inspiring experience yet. It is a testament to my personal growth and resilience, demonstrating that I can navigate the complexities of bipolar disorder without resorting to substances. My art continues to evolve, mirroring the beauty I have found in the world and within myself. The world I see is surreal. Despite the harshness of the realty, I know more than I would like to, I view life through a lens of cumulus clouds and dissociative thought patterns.

My journey is far from over, and I look forward to the new experiences and emotions that will continue to inspire my art. Sobriety has empowered me to be a better artist, one who uses her work to capture the essence of life, from its deepest struggles to its most profound beauty. In embracing sobriety, I have learned that I never needed substances to create art; I needed only the courage to confront my emotions and express them truthfully through my work.

I am Blackbird, the artist who embraces life and transforms it into art, and this journey is far from over.

Chapter 6

Subjected To Futility

I have always been the kind of person who romanticized the darker aspects of life, an outcast, lost in the world of grunge music and unreachable dreams. I would paint myself as a misunderstood teenager, hidden away in my room, surrounded by the fantastical remnants of childhood, even though I had outgrown them years ago. This part of my story is as raw and real as it gets. No sugarcoating, no glorification—just the truth.

After everything that had happened, I started going to a prestigious Catholic college. It was a place that held sacred the art of discipline, where nuns ruled with an iron fist. As a young, impressionable girl, I was thrown into this world of rigid rules and dogmatic teachings. I found myself drowning in the overwhelming pressures, struggling to keep up with the expectations. And as time passed, my darkness grew.

To understand the state of mind I was in, picture a lost young adult, still young enough to have some hope for the future yet old enough to be disillusioned by a life of mediocrity. In my world, being 'average' was an aspiration, and standing out or being unique was considered embarrassing.

I did not understand myself. I fell deeper and deeper into depression and drugs. Unable to articulate the suffocating despair that engulfed me, but my parents sensed something was terribly wrong. They called my psychiatrist, because I had tried to kill myself. They should have just left me alone. My mom and dad picked me up the next day and took me home.

After leaving, I enrolled at at a university near my home. To support my college life, I took a job at Pier One. Little did I know that the demons of addiction would soon creep into my world. I stole money from the cash register to feed my growing hunger for substances, buying marijuana in the darkest corners of the parking lot.

The recklessness of my actions reached new heights when I was caught shoplifting at Bloomingdale's. My uncle was called to rescue me, and it was a lesson that I had to learn—the painful consequences of my actions that came with it.

The transition to graduate school on a full teaching fellowship brought both challenges and opportunities. I began dating a guy. Being bisexual, I had dated both men and women, but it was with him that I would face a life-altering moment. I was an anomaly, at least in my own head. I believed I was in love, but only inside my mind. Together, my lovers and I concocted impossible, unattainable dreams.

We thought we were invincible, challenging the very fabric of reality. We had lay on the edge of his bed, staring at a big window that led to nowhere. I had many different lovers, but he stuck out.

Who knew that he would end up getting me pregnant? A drug-addicted, barely functioning adult cannot have a child. I was just a child myself. I knew he would not be much help. He was just the one who knocked me up.

At the time, I was deeply engrossed in the study of Guided Imagery, a therapeutic modality that seemed so distant from my reality. Pregnancy was not a part of my plans, so I decided to choose abortion. Why is it that women are guilted for choosing their lives over the lives of an unborn fetus? What the doctor told me had driven me to my breaking point. It was time for me to put my depression into action and make my exit from this world.

I simply took a razor and slashed my wrists open. Nice and bloody. Did not want to make a clean exit. It did not suit me. As the blood pooled around my wrists, I waited for life to slip away. However, the university therapist interrupted my perfect reverie. Someone called her.. You cannot even die in peace. Slashing your wrists does not happen as it does in the movies. You do not just keel over dramatically; it is a gradual process. At first, you become fuzzy, then an overwhelming sense of calm washes over you, and the world seems to cradle you gently. You get lost in your own thoughts and turn numb as the world fades away.

In all my near-death experiences, I have always seen a garden with bright lights, yearning to walk beyond them but always being pulled back. This time was no different. I saw angels beckoning towards me, but some "horrible human" brought me back to life. I was told I did not die that night. I was rushed to the hospital. They took me in.

I was forced onto a gurney, bright lights above me, and in my hazy state, I reached for his hand. He held it, and I passed out.

Suicide is not glamorous; it is painful, ugly, and messy. It is not about ending your life; it is a desperate cry for attention. My reasons may have seemed valid, but can there ever be a good enough reason to end one's life?

I knew I could not bring a child into the world in my fragile state. The decision to terminate the pregnancy was not made lightly, and it left me with scars that would last a lifetime. The day of the abortion is etched into my memory. The doctor who performed the procedure coldly said, "I hope you learned your lesson," as he walked past me and left the room. The plastic bag containing the remnants of what could have bore a baby was covered with a single drop of blood, a painful reminder of the choice I had made. I could not help but feel the weight of judgment from those around me.

The trauma from that experience sent me spiraling into a nervous breakdown. I sought solace in the arms of many graduate school students, hurting not only myself but others around me. It was a desperate attempt to fill the void left by the abortion and the judgment I felt from society. Eventually, I found myself in a therapist's office, who decided it was time to intervene.

I was taken to a mental hospital, a place where I could begin the process of healing. The road to recovery was long and arduous, but it was a necessary journey. I had learned the hard way that my actions had consequences, and I had to confront the darkness within me. In the years that followed, I chose to replace the void in my life with animals. I have always believed that all dogs are angels sent to guide us, and I have come to see my dogs as my children.

That experience of motherhood, in a different form, brought me a sense of purpose and healing that I desperately needed. The pregnancy was terminated when I was just 21, and I never had children after that. The scars remained, but with time and therapy, I learned to carry them as a reminder of the lessons I had learned. I had to come to terms with the fact that my choices had consequences, and the judgment of others could not define my worth. I tried to take my own life. It is never worth it.

I took it as a sign that something needed to change, a reflection of the mistakes I have made, the pain I have endured, and the growth that came from it. In the aftermath, there was regret. Regret about what I might have missed if I had succeeded, the life events I would have never experienced: I would have never experienced graduating from college or spending time with my dogs. I would have missed out on making new, close friends or meeting a worthy love. I would have missed out on so much art and creativity. Most importantly, I would not have discovered hope. Today, for the first time in a long while, I do not feel like my life is devoid of purpose.

I believe that my existence holds potential and that I do not have to burn out like a tragic French actress. The world is a series of temporary waves, and even when you feel like you have nothing to live for, there is always the next moment to look forward to – that tiny atom of change that can shake up your life in unexpected and wonderful ways. Have faith in that wacky atom and be patient, as I have been.

Chapter 7

The Final Act Of Redemption

The traumas and pain, my fallouts settled like ashes, clinging to the ruins of what I once called a life. Each day was a struggle to keep the fragments from cutting too deep, but the wounds persisted. Blackbird, the woman with hopeful eyes looking to find a life like the one in her art, colorful and vibrant, was now just a shadow, a lifeless, colorless shadow, navigating the debris of her own destruction.

Addicted to drugs made it extremely normal for me to take the hard pills of life, as normal as an everyday chore. We In my battle against life, finding a will to survive, a reason to continue my life, I found myself revolving around doors of people who never stick around. People that I thought were my close ones, the ones I would go off limits for, pushed me far away as if my call for help was a disease so contagious that if they heard me out, the past traumas and the suffering I endured would be transferred to them.

In the mess of tackling my ravenous beasts, eating me inside, getting on my mind, ready to destroy me at any moment, I realized something important—it was me, my own silent supporter, standing right there with me all along. I unleashed my power and picked myself up, faced the tragic moments that happened, and figured out a way to move forward. Instead of hiding from reality and escaping it, I needed to learn from the mistakes I made, a war between me and the darkness I was stuck in.

My sessions with my therapist were like the light to my darkness, a pathway to give life to my long-lost hopes. Finally, I figured that my past mistakes and people's thoughts on them do not define me. Talking to my therapist about everything I went through helped me heal myself. .

In the quiet moments, when my fallout leveled off, I had the time to figure out my own strength. I felt like a bird coming back to life after everything burned down. I faced the harmful stuff in my past and became stronger because of it. A phoenix rising from the ashes. In the choice to undergo an abortion, my shoulders bore the weight of others' judgments.

Better late than never, I learned that my life is worth more than people's judgment. Getting back my hopes and bringing colors to my life by finding happiness in my children and my dogs. I gave life another chance. As easy as it seemed to get back on my feet, it was ten times more difficult. I tried distancing myself from drugs but saw myself just luring more towards them all over again.

This time, I made sure I would not disappoint myself all over again. Carrying a wide smile, *fake indeed*, I stepped out to face the world, ready to carry all the toxicity it had saved for me. Little did I know I had to be stronger than I am to deal with the negativity of the world. As I moved through the world, the burden of disapproval rested heavily on my shoulders, like an invisible shroud of collective opinions.

Whispers and sidelong glances became a constant companion, a reminder that personal choices can be subjected to the harsh judgment of a society quick to give their opinions of things they never knew the depth of.

My university left no crumbs when making my healing process a nightmare. Every one of them made sure I was reminded of my dark past. I was called the worst thing anyone could have said. I was referred to as a murderer just because I couldn't save my child's life, not birthing him to a mom who was a drug addict, an university student who was prepared to commit suicide at any time because she loathed every aspect of herself.

Ignoring everything they said, I knew I was just a human being with reasons of my own that led me to where I am today, but nobody cared to look at it. I continued my day, listening to comments gradually thrown at me. Thief, drug addict, murderer, and whatnot. I kept telling myself it was okay, and their words did not define me, but deep in the back of my head, I wanted to shout my heart out and tell them I was a young child who saw her parents get divorced! From a family filled with deep trauma that I TOO INHERITED!!!

Every day, I waited for the day to end so that I could rush to my therapist and speak my heart out. The only one who cared to listen to my hurtful cries, a place where I was not judged, a place where I was given a voice, a chance to explain myself. The only place where I would feel a little more healed, a little happier, and a little stronger than I was the day before.

It was my happy place. I was entirely transparent with my therapist to find the missing pieces that I had to fill in to be better. Talking had been extremely helpful as I could see exactly where I lacked, what I did do that caused such a disaster, and what I could have done to make it better. All these questions gave me an understanding of myself and helped me learn things I never should repeat.

All the words I heard daily would vanish, and a sense of faith in myself would evolve, encouraging me to hold my head up and face the world as I was stronger and bigger than the hopeless Blackbird that I used to be. The Blackbird that they knew was now dead.

It was a cycle. Each day, I was torn, and each day, I would try to keep it together. The only beautiful thing was learning how to walk around carrying the scars of my dark past, cutting me deeper and deeper every day. It was something new for me. I would mostly escape and run away from my wounds and cries by drowning myself in the shadows of drugs, escaping reality, and enjoying my moments alone, hiding the pain I had filled in my heart.

This was different: struggling through life yet smiling wide and standing my ground to face any challenge, finding my happiness within. It was empowering. It is not that I completely stopped my use of drugs. I was an addict. These pills, like enchanting whispers, summoned me even when my heart resisted. It felt as if an unseen force, a magnetic pull, drew me in, and I found myself gliding toward them, powerless to resist. I promised myself only to use them when fighting this feeling got harder.

I tried not to be hard on myself and give myself the time to heal. I was proud of how far I had come, from being the person who once wanted to kill herself to the person who was ready to battle everything that came in front. This journey was about finding myself., going through the confusing parts of who I am. It felt like going through a big adventure. This was about changing for the better, making a promise to myself to be stronger and better and not let the past repeat itself. The dark times, which once used to be scary, became something that helped me to become tougher. With each breath I took, I took control of my life again.

My family was a complete mess. Everybody, including my grandfather, uncles, and aunt, had a heartbreaking tale to tell. It's all genetic. My mother married my dad when she was just 20 years old. My dad's family was not rich; everyone thought the only reason my dad wanted to marry my mother was her wealth. They even hired a detective to investigate whether my father was truthful in his love or not. They found out that my father had lost all his money and really loved my mom. Only then were they married. Their wedding was the "talk of the town."

My mother was a smoker, exactly like my dad, and also suffered from cancer of the thyroid gland. She was not the most beautiful woman, but my dad still loved her. My closest relative, died of Alzheimer's.

It was a mess, and now I am a mess. A mess who is trying as hard as she can to pick up her little shattered pieces and pull herself together from the trauma of the world. Every time I stayed strong, telling myself that the past is just the past and I can be better, my mind performs the very creepy act against me where it reaches my deepest darkest time, finds the worst memory, and keeps it right in front of me tearing my soul all over again. Even my mind is against me, just like the others, my worst enemy. I felt alone, wandering to find my light, my light of hope.

Little by little, every day, I get new tragic memories that flash back. It is like little episodes of Blackbird's ugly times, Episodes that had more control over my mind than I ever had. Just like every other day, I had this memory of last year that flashed when I had almost died.

He was my boyfriend, my lover, and a poet when I was 20 years old. We were tripping on some good acid. It felt magical as if I were in heaven. I heard heaven was a place for good people in the afterlife; I clearly was not from them, but it felt so real. My fingers were connected to the threads of every molecule in the stars and galaxy. I could see them all; beautiful. Just in seconds, I was on the train. A pitch black train. As scared as I should have been, I was not. I felt like I was traveling somewhere and curious to reach the unknown destination the train. was taking me to.

As soon as I thought I had reached my destination. I saw myself in a car! A car driven by two young blonde men. No longer magical or fun, It was now terrifying as if my life was in the hands of the two men, and anytime soon, I would be abducted and killed. Gladly, my life was not too good to be lived, so I had no problem being killed.

As dark as life was, my death would be even darker, A murder! Kidnapped?! Abducted?! What was I even thinking? Life has never gone my way. Why would it now?! The two young men who I thought would kill me were suddenly on the beach near an ocean. As much as I wanted death, I was just as scared, so I ran: my only opportunity to escape.

I had no wallet, no ID, and I could not even remember my name. What a shame. Somehow, early in the morning, I found myself on a road close to the boardwalk. I had no idea what to do. All I remember was that someone called the police; the only thing I could recall was my uncle's telephone number. Fortunately, he picked me up, and my magical world tour with a terrifying ending finally came to an end. He dropped me in the city, where I lived with my mother. I did not know what exactly happened and how I ever ended up on the road until years later when my uncle finally decided to tell me. This acid trip was life-changing. The moment I felt this was it; life was at the edge, and the only thing left to do was someone to push me off the edge, and I would never return.

My favorite uncle died horribly on Alzheimer's. He could not swallow at the end. His family took care of him at home. He and I would often discuss our beliefs and argue. He said that he would choose suicide with a gun when he chose to die, and I would want to use drugs, opiates, my drug of choice. I eventually gave up on suicidal ideation 9/1/22.

As much as I wished it would end for me, I still frowned, a sense of disappointment building up guilt inside me, telling me what I was even doing with my life. I was ruining my own life with my bare hands, drowning myself deeper into the dark and wasting my precious years. Without that acid trip, I would have never gotten back to finding my hope, my light, and crawling myself out of the darkness. I would have never understood it was only I who could save myself. My life was not about giving up or seeing the clock tick until it was finally my end time. With every fall, I promised to rise because I deserved to live the best, and with every frown that life brings, I will create happiness for myself because I deserve redemption. all the smiles and laughter in the world.

Chapter 8

To Light And Darkness

On my journey to discover my lost self, bandaging my own wounds until they were slit deeper by the words of people that continue to haunt me till my last breath, for the decisions that I made, that too for my personal well-being affected people who had nothing to do with. I was no longer a human to them but a gossip, a topic they found fun to talk about.

My traumatizing life was nothing more than a joke to them. They found it fun to mock me and remind me of my dark times; maybe they had nothing interesting to do in their life that made them so involved in mine; I feel pity for them. But do I? Their boisterous laughs and giggles, wide smiles across their faces, were everything I asked for from the start. Something that I was never blessed with, but I had to look for it myself from anywhere I could.

As hard as life was, my time with the therapist did help a lot; even then, people from all walks of life made sure to leave no crumbs in making life harder. When I went through my abortion, I had a severe nervous breakdown from everything that went on around me and not being able to control myself; with all the taunts and thoughts that rushed through me, I could not hold on any longer and decided this was it, I quit on life.

Adrenaline rushed through my veins, and sizzling chills ran down my body as a sense of rage took over me; regrets engulfed my trembling soul as I grabbed the blade I had saved in my bag and slit my wrist once and for all. Blood swamped out my half-slit wrist with all the feelings I had buried in my torn soul. I felt a sense of relief seeing it all end. and I no longer had to face any of the challenges anymore. That is how my story ends. My eyes slowly began shutting down, and I felt my soul leaving my body. This was it, my end.

I once read that we only have a total of five liters of blood in us. I know for sure I was in the bathroom for exactly five whole minutes, yet they were not enough to drain all my blood off my body. Even failed at the attempt to kill myself. Is there anything I might even succeed at? Oh yes, having the worst of life and luck indeed, I top at it. My eyes opened in a hospital room, lying in bed. I looked over to my wrist, which I had cut just a few minutes ago, it was bandaged, and I was alive. How much more could I disappoint myself?

My therapist had admitted me to a mental hospital after my attempt to kill myself. I was trying hard to turn myself as hard as the concrete beneath my feet, but the people could not understand, and I could not keep on pushing myself any further. I accepted the reality all around me and agreed to try and treat myself in the mental hospital as if I had any other options left.

That is just how cruel life is. It changes you from within at times. My first days at the mental hospital were nothing less than traumatic. I felt like there was so much wrong with me that I was not able to fix. I knew I wanted to get my life back together, and I promised to rise back up every time I fell because I deserved to be happy, but being in the hospital made me feel the opposite of all the strength I had finally gained to be better. I felt like I did not deserve to live, and the world would be better off without me. I was a burden. Nothing seemed to work out.

I was diagnosed with bipolar disorder, a chronic mental illness that answered all the questions I had in my head. The mixed emotions I felt, wanting to quit on life, the thoughts and episodes I came across were all the consequences of one single thing: my mental illness. For once, I was happy, having faith that I would be treated and all the problems in my life would finally come to an end, and after I was cured, I could finally be happy.

But hopes, they are always just hopes, aren't they? And nothing more. At the hospital, they say we care for you and want you to do better, but they are all just a bunch of lies they tell you. Instead, they do not care whether you are healed or not. They just torture you at level where there is not much we can really do. That is just how I felt; there was nothing that I could do by myself. I had no control over anything; not even the smallest desires or needs were taken care of. I could not do anything of my own will. I was controlled entirely, and if I did not wish to do something, I was tortured to work all day. Tirelessly. My anger had grown to a much higher level that every little thing triggered me, which always resulted in relapse .

I never had the experience of making friends. I was the kid who loved being alone at all costs; happiness was never something I experienced, and I did not know how it felt like until I numbed myself with a high dose of drugs. However, I did manage to make one friend in the hospital which was shocking. I know. You would not be shocked to hear the fact that the only reason I was friends with this girl was because she had her sources of drugs. I could get them from her whenever I wanted. Part of me wanted to heal my inner self, but sometimes it would get really stressful, and I could not push myself further.

I would usually get feedback for not being able to control my anger or my emotions. I felt that the rules were way too strict. for me to handle. I could not escape, and neither could I survive. All that I could do was accept everything the way it was, and that is exactly what I began doing.

My faith in God grew stronger when I was in the Rampo Ridge mental hospital. I saw the God of light, which made me curious about the angels. I started studying the existence of angels, and I started believing that life would finally be better. I always believed in God when I was young, but I started doubting as I got older.

Now, seeing and understanding the existence of God and his angels has made me feel better about myself. I started following rules as much as I could and trusting God. But the drugs, I could not control myself on drugs. There were times when I was caught getting high in the washroom several times and was sent to rehab. This is when I finally decided I did not want to continue living my life, escaping from anything I felt discomforting; rather, I would find the positivity that surrounded me, and with all the positive energy along with my trust in God, I would start again. It was hard at first, but I reminded myself of the beautiful life that I wished for, and I could only get that if I started fixing myself, I would make myself strong enough to deal with the world that tried its utmost to bring me down in any way it could.

I started taking therapy seriously and made up my mind to figure out everything I lacked and fix myself once and for all. I was given a bundle of medications every day to detox drugs. I started taking my stay in the mental hospital positively and cooperated with the doctors and my therapist.

Each day, I would go through a new episode that would make me challenge my existence. My mind had a habit of playing tricks whenever it could. My episodes started increasing due to my bipolar disorder. The medications I was on would only detoxify me, but I needed something to numb me entirely. My only escape was my drugs, but I did not want to escape; I wanted to face my reality and challenge my episodes, control my anger, and keep myself focused on my goal to live the life I deserved. A life that contained all the happiness I could never have.

Every day was me fighting the demons that haunt me, struggling to wake up, terrified I might have another episode, scared to face it all over again, yet I have nowhere to go, nowhere to hide from the demons that live inside me. Struggling to figure out who I really was? Is this me? Or am I the demon that roars inside me? Who am I?

I had episodes where I could not sleep for two days straight and felt extremely sad, even when there was nothing to be upset over.

When I heard about the death of my closest friend, the amount of sorrow I should have felt I did not; instead, I had yet another episode where I was thrilled and energetic about the news, and I knew it was not me. Later, when my episode ended, I felt an immense amount of pain in my chest hearing the loss of someone beloved.

I lost my entire self, yet I believed that I would be okay and would get in control of it, slowly and gradually. I had been in rehab for a good amount of time and slowly got in control of my usage of drugs until I had the biggest episode I could not ever have, and making myself numb was the only option left. I had no control over my thoughts and felt everything I did was entirely useless.

I heard voices telling me I would never be any better than the kind of person I was, I did not deserve happiness. Everything got worse when I heard yet another voice in my head that was like the voice of a fetus, calling me a murderer and whispering that I killed him; I was a bad mother who never deserved happiness because I killed my own kid.

That is when I heard my heart shattering into millions of pieces, my soul tearing apart all over again. I felt hopeless; my hands dropped from my ears to my sides, showing that I had lost. I took a bunch of pills I had left and took them all at once and laid hopelessly on the bed. I could not handle the voices any further. I wanted them to stop, at least for now.

I had a relapse the following day and still felt numb. The only thing I remembered was that one voice still in my mind as loud as it was yesterday. I told my therapist, still numb, about everything that happened yesterday. She comforted me and gave me the hope to try again. Maybe this was it; that is what my life Is now. Me, I was on a battle against myself, each day facing a new challenge to find the happiness that I knew I deserved.

Chapter 9

Gods And Ghosts

I always said "I have nothing." I am largely self-taught with a few photography courses with Patt Blue and Via Wynroth at ICP in NYC and at the New School with George Tice. In 1972, I received a B.A. in psychology and was later granted a master's teaching fellowship at a university in their existential phenomenology psychology program.

In the bustling town of Teaneck, New Jersey, I worked as a cashier at Pier One, a store renowned for its eclectic import and export goods. This role was a stark later contrast to my academic endeavor, where I held a teaching fellowship in existential phenomenology. The subject matter often delved into profound areas, including the sensitive topic of abortion.

My journey also led me to Southampton, New Jersey, where I juggled four waitress jobs at various establishments: a discotheque named Jaws, a steakhouse, and a diner. The camaraderie among the staff was palpable; we were a close-knit group of artists and kindred spirits who would often congregate at the diner after hours. It was there that I served everyone, but the long hours on my feet took their toll, resulting in varicose veins that threatened my mobility. Seeking change, I ventured to a mental hospital in Schenectady, New Jersey, lured by a fascination with a man named Oscar who had interviewed me. However, the job proved overwhelming as I struggled to connect with a particular client and grappled with my own demons as a low-bottom alcoholic. My life became a cycle of drinking to muster the courage to work and then drinking to forget the day's toils. I resided at the YWCA in Schenectady, New York, where my roommates concocted red rock candy in the kitchen, and I drank myself into oblivion nightly. On one occasion, Oscar sought to take me out on a date, but I could not bear to face him or the world outside, so I ignored the persistent ring to my room, despite hearing it clearly.

The following day, I confided in Oscar that my time at the mental hospital had come to an end. I proposed a new endeavor: to seek out a residence for the patients transitioning from the temporary facility. After a diligent search, I discovered an ideal home and promptly informed Oscar of the find. With that task complete, I announced my departure to return to the city to be with my mother.

I resided with my mother, setting foot on a journey toward sobriety.

In due course, I secured employment at Georgetown Systems. The company's president, upon our first meeting, offered me a position. There was an undeniable mutual attraction, despite his marital status, which puzzled me at the time. The reason behind this would later become clear. Six months into my tenure, he revealed plans to expand with a new office in, New Jersey. He envisioned a weekly publication listing job opportunities for clients and proposed that I spearhead this project as its editor, even offering to finance my relocation to New Jersey for six months. My task was to assemble a team of 16 copy editors to scour The New York Times and other regional newspapers for potential listings. After a thorough recruitment process, I enlisted a cadre of exceptional college graduates, among whom I appointed an experienced woman as my deputy editor.

The publication flourished. During this period, I lived in an attic apartment. My affinity for attic spaces was well-known; I enjoyed such a dwelling with Tom & Karen, and their two daughters, capturing our moments together through photography. Tragically, after my departure, Karen succumbed to breast cancer at a young age.

It was then that the president of Georgetown Systems made his intentions clear. He requested my company on a business trip to California, an invitation laden with implications. I declined, out of respect for his wife, whom I held in high regard. His subsequent offer of a promotion left me conflicted. Despite my fondness for the job, I doubted my capabilities to do it. Ultimately, I chose to resign. My true passion lay in photography and art, pursuits I wished to dedicate myself to fully, even if it meant indulging in substances like cocaine, Percocet, marijuana, and Quaaludes. My lover introduced me to an alternative in vodka, a substitute that seemed safer and more accessible. One fateful day, we ventured to the city in search of Quaaludes, a decision that would mark a significant turn in my life's journey.

Chapter 10

Abstract Creative Force

I have tried and had, by far, all the drugs I could find, from psychedelics all the way to cocaine. Also had marijuana, but no drug has been as harmful to my health as the drug of love. Love has to be the worst kind of drug I have ever had. Nevertheless, it is an addiction, and knowing how much I might suffer when I have it, it is just as much needed. Like all the other drugs, it is extremely beautiful at the beginning, but deep in the depths, it only cut my soul deeper. Something I do to myself every once in a while, the only kind of drug that tops all levels of pain I might have ever felt.

Love is where I find peace, but a kind of peace that only lasts for a small amount of time; what follows is the worst kind of pain, wounds far more difficult to heal and time-consuming. Wounds that might even be life-long, the pain might become easier to handle, but it is only us who know deep inside how much those wounds still hurt.

Love is a word so beautiful, a feeling so mesmerizing, yet filled with toxic death following. A death we ourselves ask for, a death we know will occur, yet let it engulf us all over again. That is exactly what I did with my life. I am bisexual and have been in multiple relationships all my life, all including the good and bad. I have also had one-night stands and been in a threesome relationship. A pretty mixed-up life ...an entire mess!

Being young, I was confused about the weird feeling I had toward women, the kind of feeling I should have had for a guy; I never felt it; instead, all those emotions rose up all at once for the women in my school. It took me long enough to identify that I was not really interested in guys, and my heart felt more attracted to women.

I was scared to acknowledge this when young and would always find myself covered in guilt whenever I was close to my friends. It was painful to feel that way, covered in guilt and confusion, I was unable to figure out the feelings and emotions filled in me.

The girl from high school I fell in love with, every time I saw her pass me a smile, my heart felt a satisfaction I never felt anywhere else.

Her bright blue eyes perfectly complimented her beautiful coffee-like brown hair that she waved off whenever they came near her eyes. I would always think if she even smelled like coffee, she did. Her skin was as fair as milk, with freckles bringing the prettiest tan to exist, and if that was not it, she even had a dimple across one side of her face. In short, she was breathtaking. My heart stopped every time she took her hair, pulled it up, rolled it in a bun, and tied it with the scrunchie she had in her hand. Everything she did was filled with grace; it was mesmerizing.

I never had the confidence to talk to her, even after having the advantage of being a girl. What I did, in fact, was use this advantage and be best friends with her best friend. For the first time in a long time, my luck worked out in my favor, and she, too, was interested in me. She was the first girl I dated. In fact, my very first relationship was with her.

A beautiful soul that was ripped apart in pieces just like me. We had so much in common, like our hatred for people, our hope for a better life, and a bit of luck that never sided with us. If all these things were not enough, another habit that we had in common was numbing ourselves when in pain. She was exactly like me. It was like a dream come true, watching the girl I liked being the first person to understand my feelings and everything I go through, the things that I do, the decisions I take, the feelings buried in me she would feel, appreciate, and understand it all.

She would tell me everything she went through, and I would tell her I was by her side and understood her feelings. We would bash people, laugh, and to numb the pain we felt, we would drug ourselves and sit on the rooftop of the school until we passed out. Just as much as we liked each other, instead of making ourselves happy and thinking good for each other, we would numb and harm our health, but these were the only moments we felt content, moments when we were together, moments when I told myself I was the happiest person alive.

But was I? Just a little amount of happiness made me forget that life was never fair to me. How did I forget that luck never worked my way? It was only there to play games with my heart. You were in love with an addict.

Just after a few months, she started being distant; she would no longer sit with me on rooftops nor share her hard times with me anymore. My heart ached to see her gradually parting ways. I had never felt that feeling in my life; it is even harder to put into words; no words could bring justice to the kind of pain I felt. Whenever my heart pounded for her, I saw her fleeing further away. The only way I could define this feeling is it was gut-wrenching and distressing. I felt distorted.

She began feeling attracted to her best friend, who, in turn, was attracted to me. My relationship with her turned into timely hookups between her best, me, and she. A threesome just after my first relationship. It took me long enough to get over her, and she played a huge role in it.

Getting over her made me try things I never thought I would. Each day, I would be out spending most of my time being high and not wanting to live life or feel any pain I encountered. The rest of the time, I would cry myself until all the hurt I felt would not sweep away. I stopped seeing my family to escape from the everyday drama and even ended up in a one-night stand with a girl. Eventually, I began losing myself and wasting my life crying for a girl who no longer wanted me. Eventually, realized I was only making a fool out of myself, and it was not even worth it.

As hurtful as breaking up with her was, I ended up in a relationship just a few months later. I felt like being with men would be better, and I would feel more fulfilled rather than being hurt by a woman. I began dating him, who was in my university. He was a guy who liked me long enough, but I never seemed to notice him. In the case of seeking attention from the people who never thought of us, not even once, we overlooked, under appreciated, and eventually lost the people who genuinely care for us.

How naïve can we human beings be to believe what we want is the best for us?

On my chase to get attention from Amy, only to hurt and shatter myself entirely, I overlooked the man who kept trying his best just to have a word with me. I instantly felt a calming feeling that stitched the wounds she left for me. In every drop of the five-liter blood in my body, I felt a wave of contentment whenever he would tell me how much he liked and wanted me. Although I was not really attracted to guys, being with him did make me believe that dating guys was, in fact, way better, or was it? He was the best kind of guy I might have ever met.

Just being with him gave me hope that I do, in fact, deserve happiness. His love for me filled my long-lost craving; I started feeling better about myself. He went all ways just to make me happy, whether it was just listening to my hardest times or comforting me in a way that would instantly make my dull day brighten up, making me laugh on the moments I wanted to cry, hugging me in the moments I felt alone, he was everything I ever needed, when sad, he would always buy flowers just to tell me he was proud of me for making it through today, just him being there was enough; but again, naïve human beings.

Like any other day, the same darkness would revolve around me, instantly fading as soon as he stepped in and sat next to me on the rooftop. Gazing at the stars and admiring the beauty of the full moon was our favorite moment together. It was like the sweet, small spot we had where we shared the hard truths of life.

 Knowing we could be extremely transparent when around each other without fear of being judged and how he made me comfortable whenever I was near him was my favorite and the most memorable thing about him; everything I need now. Sitting next to me on the rooftop, seeing my teary eyes, he brought his hand close to my face, tucked the loose strand of my hair behind my ear, and wiped out my tears as they kept dripping from my eyes.

What I regretted the most was that I never felt attracted to him in any sort of way; his touch felt meaningless, absolutely nothing, dry and dead as if the loss of her had made me bury all my emotions. Even if that were it, I would have been happy and okay, but what was even worse was that being the naïve human being I was, I still wanted her attention. Just looking at her made my heart skip a beat. The emotions I had never felt for him, I kept feeling for anyone but just not him.

It began getting hard to manipulate myself into thinking I liked him when he was only just a friend that I wanted in my life. The feeling grew stronger, and I began distancing myself from him. Knowing exactly how hard it might be for him, I overlooked it. The only thing I really cared about was me. This is one night, when I was alone distancing myself from him, I ended up having a one-night stand with Cathy Moda, which resulted in my breakup with a guy so good I could have never deserved him.

When I was in the midst of getting more acquainted to new drug substances, I met a guy, a poet, an artist, and an alcoholic. Being with him was the first time I had alcohol. Weirdly enough, I was the one attracted to him. A tall, masculine man with a fine beard dressed like the one from dreams, at least for me, a complete hot mess! Exactly the kind of man I like.

It is strange how all the close people in my life that I ever encountered do drugs; anyone I meet is always someone who has the source of drugs; it was as if the universe was guiding me towards it, and I was happy with my use of drugs. Or was it my boundaries that were never set and would only further lead me to like the same kind of people? It was an unsolved puzzle.

He was the guy I had experienced the worst kind of acid trip where I almost died. Not knowing where I was and who I was with, even after being completely conscious, I still did not remember anything that happened that day, nor did I ever know where he went. Tragic.

The guy I met in the university, the man who made me pregnant: Just like all the others, he never stayed long but made sure my life was entirely ruined. The worst kind of relationship I have ever had, a man so toxic, leaving lifelong wounds that would never heal, wounds that still haunt me to my core, wounds that killed me alive, leading me to take my life. How could someone be this horrific to ruin someone's life forever knowingly? Steve proved it how!

A man, whom I met on Facebook. He was married but separated from his wife. He had covid. When in the hospital, he said he wanted to come to live with me. They lived in CA.

I was in a mental hospital when I thought he had come to me, but he never did. Disappointed and failed at love. At times when I needed love the most, it was never there. He will forever be missed – the best non harmful drug that ever existed.

The last few years has taught me that when it is my time to leave this body no one can stop it. We have one life to live. The material things we invest in are left behind only to be discarded.

I went to a therapist for 12 years. For the better part of a year, we spent each session talking about my dysfunction. We never talked about her dysfunction. We had about 11 more sessions.. He said the problem was that it always takes two to tango and we never talked about her dance moves. All we did was talk about me.

The therapist had a sign outside his office saying, "CURING PEOPLE WITH KINDNESS."

The problem with that statement was that he was taking about his kindness. You had to keep going to him and talking to him to stay well. You had to talk to him each week, tell him all your problems and he would give his kind and loving ear for you to face life and go on. He never asked you to change. He gave placebo advice and platitudes. If you had serious and significant childhood trauma, he had nothing to offer you but how he dealt with his own serious childhood trauma. How deep was his trauma? How deep did it go? A therapist can only give what they have. No human being can give what they do not have.

Each human being has to, in the final analyses, must pick herself up by her own bootstraps. Nobody can do that for you. Nobody. Not even God. You must do the inner work first, to receive God's help. Until then, you are dependent on the kindness of strangers, family and friends for as long as they can or will give of themselves to keep you afloat.

Chapter 11

Flourish

Joseph was my favorite uncle on my mother's side. A staunch atheist and a World War II veteran, he led a life marked by both conflict and beauty. He married a stunning woman, and together they created a picturesque family, blessed with two children. Their daughters, were like younger cousins to me, growing up to be beautiful young women in their own right. Their elder daughter had a genuine appreciation for my work, their younger daughter did too. They, postponing marriage to focus on their lives, which were now painted in a glorious tableau amidst the ongoing chaos of human conflict.

In our discussions, Uncle Joseph often mused about the futility of war and the possibility of its end. He once claimed the right to end his own life if he so chose. I resonated with his sentiment until September 11, 2022, when I relinquished my own thoughts of suicide and entrusted my life to the care of a higher power. This divine presence, which I envisioned as a mother who birthed the entire universe starting with the Big Bang, seemed to guide the universe's grand narrative. The James Webb Telescope, a remarkable investment by NASA and European scientists, ventured into the cosmos with its enormous golden wings, uncertain of its success. Yet it did succeed, marking a significant leap in our understanding of the universe.

Uncle Joseph and his family often gathered to discuss current affairs, religion, and philosophy. While he, his children, and his side of the family were atheists, his wife and her mother were not. My uncle's discussions were vibrant with the exchange of ideas about political science, religion, and philosophical thought. He and I came to an agreement that it was best to let God, in all her infinite wisdom, decide the manner and timing of my final rest. When the time came, I envisioned walking through a door, flinging it open to find God, the Mother of all Time.

Nearby lived Nancy, a compassionate friend dedicated to suicide prevention. As her husband battled cancer, Nancy's unwavering care kept him alive. We bonded over our shared belief in euthanasia, a concept not yet legal in New Jersey. On September 11, 2022, I decided to surrender my suicidal ideations and instead spent the day with Lambchop my faithful companion. Although my home felt too vast and empty, Lambchop seemed content on her little pillow.

Upon returning home with Lambchop, I found a tiny stuffed Lambchop, a gift from my sister, waiting for us. My real Lambchop, weighing just five pounds, curled up in a small Chinese pillow I used at my desk. She was underweight, infested with fleas and mites, and her teeth were in poor condition. I felt a pang of guilt as I looked at her sad eyes but tried to provide comfort as we settled back into our home.

Uncle Peter, a renowned painter of desert scenes, portraits, and landscapes, had never married and lived alone in a beautiful home. His portraits were well sought after, allowing him a comfortable life. When we visited him, he would be dressed in a three-piece suit, smoking cherry-flavored tobacco in a light-filled room. We shared a common addiction—nicotine. His passing left me with a few of his paintings, including a drawing of a desert scene and a watercolor landscape, which I later framed.

In my home, surrounded by the spirits of departed relatives and pets, they all feel like guardian angels. My struggle with bipolar depression consumed ten years of my life. During this time, I was unable to even walk my little Scottish Terrier, McPherson. I hired neighborhood children to take him out while I remained in bed, smoking cigarettes and watching the news, creating art from memory and dreams.

The only reprieve from my profound depression came through Electroconvulsive Therapy (ECT), both in and out of the mental hospital. The sight of mentally ill and desperate individuals in the hospital was harrowing. During the ECT sessions, I developed an addiction to propranolol, a testament to the complexities of my ongoing battle with mental health.

Chapter 12

Black Hole

When I met Laverne, she was emerging from the local halfway house, a recovering heroin addict with a past etched in hardship and hope. Her journey through recovery led her to AA meetings, where I first heard her speak. In my home, I had been renting out three bedrooms to women in similar circumstances, offering them not just rooms but a chance at redemption. I had helped many of these women find stability, helping them with their jobs and AA meetings. Taking a chance on Laverne, I offered her one of the available rooms.

Each day before Laverne took the bus to her job. Went to her job, she would leave me small, heartfelt notes on cards. They were simple yet profound, such as:

"Blackbird, have a nice day. I love you very much. I want to hold you. The prayer for us is that I may feel the divine. I pray that I will have a good time with you this week. I feel the spirit in you. You make me happy. You look very beautiful. You have a peace in yourself. You are in my soul and in my heart. Love, Laverne."

On September 11, I celebrated Laverne's one-year AA anniversary with a potluck dinner at my home. Her birthday was just a week earlier, on September 4. We transformed the space with tents, music, flowers, and candles on large round tables. A folk-rock band was scheduled to play, but when they arrived, a torrential downpour began. The band, concerned about the electrical setup, said they might have to leave. I insisted they continue, suggesting we lay wooden planks on the wet grass. Despite the weather, the music played on. My father and his second wife traveled from Florida to attend, and a bus from the halfway house brought more guests to the party.

My move to Old City, Philadelphia marked a new chapter. Adopting the name Blackbird, I received a card from Laverne congratulating me on my new home:

"Congratulations on your new nest. May it be filled with happiness. Buddy, Matt & Jeff. Happy New Year!"

On New Year's Eve, during a snowstorm, I sent for Laverne. She arrived in a cab I had paid for, carrying only a small suitcase in the midst of the storm. I had overlooked the fact that she was on parole, and if discovered, she risked returning to jail.

In Philadelphia, I had rented a converted gallery. Directly across the street was a bar that resembled the one from the sitcom Cheers. As I followed the moving company in my little red Beetle with McPherson, my Scottish Terrier, I encountered a surreal scene on Race Street—an entire circus with giraffes, ballerinas, clowns, and birds. The scene was so fantastical I wondered if it was a hallucination. Yet, it did not deter my excitement. I was elated to finally be free, soaring into the night.

"Blackbird fly, blackbird fly…"

One evening, Laverne and I attended an AA meeting in Centre City, Philly. I brought my camera and began taking photos. Laverne took the camera and my bag, and I wandered off, eventually finding a Starbucks. There, I encountered a drunk who also wanted coffee. When the attendant refused to give us coffee due to company policy, I solicited donations from other customers and bought coffee for both the drunk and myself.

Laverne eventually found me and took me back to our studio. The experience felt disorienting, as if I was in a manic state of bipolar disorder. The high was exhilarating but fleeting.

After about a month in Philadelphia, my family arrived to take me back to Princeton. I initially thought they had come for a visit and planned to show them my neighborhood. I looked forward to showing them my favorite coffee shop, which allowed dogs and computers and hosted local art shows. However, instead of a casual visit, my father, a policeman, and my sister took me to Princeton, where they had me sign a Power of Attorney. They then took me to a hospital.

Unaware of the real reason for my hospitalization, I searched for an explanation, suggesting I was giving birth to Jesus Christ. At the psychiatric hospital, I was placed in the unit known as Crazy Eddies due to my refusal of antipsychotic medication. For a week, I slept on a mattress on the floor while two men administered injections daily. Eventually, I consented to take the medication and joined the general population.

In the hospital, I found solace in creating collages. Art and music therapy proved to be profoundly healing. Laverne visited me every day. During my stay, my Philadelphia landlord sent a letter, but my family and Laverne moved me back to New Jersey without my knowledge.

Life is a series of changes—failures, recoveries, growth, and love. Through these experiences, I strive to become a better version of myself each day. I am proud of the strong, independent woman I am today and deeply grateful for the remarkable people who surround me.

When I was last in the hospital, I asked the art therapist for the tablecloths we used during art therapy sessions. Each of us had created art on the back of these plastic tablecloths, making them a collective masterpiece. She gave me two of these cloths, which I still treasure as symbols of co-created art.

On September 1, 2022, I encountered my higher power. With only a few Percocet left, I contemplated using them to escape my pain. Relying on the power of thought, which shapes our experiences and outcomes, I found myself in a confrontation with my higher power. She appeared as a brilliant white light in a black void. She revealed herself as what I had been searching for since birth and advised me to stop fixating on my reflection. She guided me to take steps two and three in AA, and to engage in prayer and meditation.

As I reflect on my journey, from the vibrant chaos of Philadelphia to the quiet comfort of home, I recognize the growth that came from each trial and triumph. My story is one of resilience and transformation, marked by the people who have been part of it— friends, family, and loved ones. Each chapter, each encounter, has shaped me into a stronger, more self-aware individual.

Chapter 13

Restrained Freedom

Blackbird:

I had a dream last night. I was in a hotel with my deceased mother (she died of heart failure at 75 years). Two male friends were sitting next to me reading National Geographic. All of a sudden, my deceased father (he died at 94 years old of cancer) stepped through a door. He was embodied and looked like he was 60 years old. He was dressed in a suit, shirt & tie. He greeted me with a gentle smile and extended his hands as if to hold mine. I said "Dad, can I feel you?" He smiled. I tried to feel him. I did. Then I woke up.

Angus:

… heavy duty dream.

Was the dream comforting, upsetting, transcendent or ambiguous?

Blackbird:

Transcendent, comforting. I look forward to sleeping again now
… the world of human beings chatters incessantly and never makes any sense unless, of course, you make sense to yourself.

How did you learn these things?

1. The first step is to know yourself.

2. The second step is to accept yourself as you are, all your zits, warts and character defects. For each defect you have, you have a redeeming quality. Accept and love yourself and you will come to accept and love other people.

3. Appreciate the beauty of nature. Nature can lay waste to humanity in the blink of an eye yet, at the same time, it is filled with majesty, wonder and beauty.

Human beings are a part of nature. Nature and the originator of nature placed us on this planet. Nature gave us our birthright. Life is a gift.

I owe it to myself to be a compassionate steward of my life. I am no less than a mighty mountain and no more than a baby deer nibbling on a piece of grass alongside its mom.

Life is a gift. Life is beautiful.

Life is what you make it.

Chapter 14

Spaces Within The World

I was born in PA, near where my grandfather built a beautiful white house with a gazebo, veranda, a well, and tennis court, before the area was developed. Every summer, my mother's family would leave their large apartment in Brooklyn to spend the season in the Mountains, where it was cooler.

My artwork focuses on memory, dreams, and personal history, combined with a love for the quiet elegance of nature. Nature's poetic form, perfect symmetry, vibrant colors, and endless mystery deeply inspire me. Since I started photographing in 1979, I have felt the need to add my own touch to the scenes I capture, often resulting in a surreal quality. For many years, I hand-colored my black-and- white silver prints and displayed this work.

I wear leg braces due to an injury, which limits my walking time. A telephoto lens allows me to "walk" with my camera. Discovering mobile photography apps was incredibly exciting for me, offering a new palette and tools for creating images. Now, I photograph with a DSLR and then import the images into my iPad and MacBook for further interpretation.

Everybody likes to say they are eclectic and are familiar with all the schools of psychology but, in reality, they have not really internalized the full implications of each theory. Their ego, IMO, gets in the way of internalizing the implications. In this sense, they are imposters. Rather than acknowledge their limitations they superficially gloss over the theories that are out of their depth and access the theories they are comfortable with and act accordingly. IMO, many psychologists do more harm than good because of this.

I went to a psychoanalytic psychotherapist 3 times a week for 4 years. Even with insurance that paid 80% of the bill, I paid a hefty sum out of pocket. There is no such thing as a free lunch; he was worth it. He knew his stuff. I benefited enormously in the relationship. He did not claim to be anything he wasn't. He was a Freudian psychoanalyst. He had little to no use for Carl Jung. Freud's theory revolved around sex. The sex drive was supreme. Freud theory discounted God completely. There is utility in Freudian psychoanalysis still it is not conducive to a power beyond the mechanics of being a physical human being beset by human instincts which bedevil human beings.

Carl Jung's theory does not negate Freud's theory. It does, however, engulf it. It is a subset. Jung's theory is more hopeful. It is all encompassing.

The AA program is about hope. Hope for the individual, hope for the group and a hope that can, potentially, transcend an asteroid smashing into our planet and catapult us into a catastrophic ice age. AA is a program that has the capacity to rise above a global nuclear war that renders humankind extinct. Life is transitory. In time, All things will pass. In time, you and I will pass away, This is a given. Billions of years from now the sun will burn itself out. Everything we worry and fret about today will not mean a goddamned thing.

Still, life is good. We are alive in this moment. We owe it to ourselves and the world about us to be what we can be. God either exists or God does not exist. If God does exist, God is all and everything. God is the good, the bad and the ugly. God is the sun, the moon and the stars. God is eternity. We like to think we are the be all and the end all. We are not. We are but a sliver of a much greater whole. A sliver is but a sliver, yet a sliver is something, nonetheless.

When. I am well, I have faith. I have hope. Life is an awe-inspiring gift. I am grateful. I have no wish to bite the hand that feeds me. My wish is to play my part, do my part, and live to the best of my ability with what nature has bestowed upon me.

I'm all in.

… don't know if I should feel flattered, complemented, worthy, unworthy, false or insulted. We, in AA, are the blind leading the blind trudging the road to happy destiny.

I would rather be a fool chasing a dream with hope in my heart rather than a nihilist staring down an abyss of darkness and despair with no hope to speak of.

Chapter 15

Illusions

I went to many mental hospitals. My first was when I was 30 years old. My AA sponsor took me there. I had told all my doctors that I was in AA. Was not diagnosed yet as a bipolar person. My doctors Wouldn't give me anything to help me sleep. So I went to drugstores to get NyQuil and drugs like that. That did not work. Eventually, after days of not sleeping, I saw cameras in my bathroom and when I stepped out of my home, all my neighbors came out of their doors

… that terrified me. I called my sponsor. She took me to the hospital there they sent me to a local mental hospital. When I realized where I was, I ran out of an open door. Imagine an open door in a mental hospital. I ran down the street, but my sponsor ran after me and tackled me to the ground and said you are going back the mental hospital … they put me on Haldol. I felt like a ghost. Eventually, the only thing I could do is play ping-pong in a big room with the other mental patients. When my sister came to visit, she did not recognize me. That is what drugs can do to a person. Now, I know I need drugs I take drugs for my bipolar illness, but they are not that strong.

Since then, I have been in many mental hospitals. In Carrier, they kept me in Crazy Eddie's for a week. It was only meant to be for patients who had gotten out of control. It was meant to be a "cooling" off time of a couple of hours. Two men would come in every day. I laid down on a mattress and they would shoot me full of antipsychotics.

After a week, they let me out. I started making collages with the soap at the nurse's station & torn magazines I drew on.

One of my mental hospitals was Northbrook. There I was told I was the God of light by another patient. I thought she was God. Her roommate taught me many valuable things about how to live. I thought I saw Jesus he wore a long robe and had a long beard he walked up and down the hallway with Ken Casey the author of one flew over the cuckoo's nest. When we went to dinner or lunch for breakfast, Jesus always sat at the head of the table. I was in a wheelchair and people would wheel me to just sit wherever there was room. Jesus helped everybody with their meals, giving them bread and coffee. People would give me bread and coffee with my eggs in the morning. There was a menu I could choose from I often did not like my dinners, but I ate them anyway. there was wonderful art & music therapy after our meals. Then someone would put a blanket over me since we were in the winter and I did not have enough clothes as I kept giving them away. Someone would wheel me into a gigantic recreation area so I could smoke cigarettes finally, I could breathe. Patients would exercise .... Playing basketball and dancing and running around a circle. I was confined to my wheelchair. But I enjoyed it anyway because I had fresh air and could smoke cigarettes. I even saw the pope. She was a woman. She told me she was not the pope but carried a Bible around all the time with her when I first got to Northbrook. My roommate was in a bad way. I felt very sorry for her. One night she could not make it to the bathroom and I cleaned up after her on my hands and knees. Then I saw that she had wonderful drawings next to her bed, and I organize them for her.

Eventually, I came to and realized that I had been hallucinating and that Jesus and the apostles were only hallucinations and that they were real people. I left that mental hospital to go to physical therapy and one of the aids helped me take a shower, even though I could not stand on my own after being in a wheelchair for so long I did not want to leave the mental hospital. I felt comfortable there but I did. When I got to physical therapy. I tried to do what they said, but soon called a friend of mine to pick me up and take me home. My sister was furious. She said I should stay there and do the physical therapy. I told everybody that physical therapy was not helping me. I just wanted to be home with my sister and my dog.

The man I called was a friend in AA who drove other AA members around for a living. I told him I did not have cash, but I would give it to him when I got home. I told him what time to pick me up, I was afraid he would not do it, but there he was at the time I had given him. My bags were packed and we proceeded home. I was exhausted when I got home. I was at Northbrook and then physical therapy for several months, but I left too soon and soon landed up in another mental hospital.. There I was called the queen. Everyone called me the queen because I was elderly and in a wheelchair and wore a big fuzzy coat. My main objective after every meal was to smoke cigarettes. There was wonderful group, art and music therapy. There I discovered that I was also a musician in one of the sessions.

Now I go to a partial hospitalization program. I have a wonderful therapist and enjoy the other patients. There I smoke cigarettes, e-cigarettes, nicotine gum & mints. This is my worst current addiction. They say that withdrawing from nicotine is worse than drawing from heroin. I think that is true.

One night I had a dream that I was with my dead mother in a room. We were sitting at a bar. Dr. Bob and Bill Wilson were sitting next to me reading something. I thought I must be dead because I was sitting near my dead mother, though I could not see her. Then all of a sudden my father came out of a door. He had died at the age of 93. He walked slowly towards me. I was astounded. He looked like he was 60 …. he was dressed in a tan suit. his face glowed. There were no words between us. He just smiled at me with infinite love and forgiveness. He reached out his hands to me. Then I said dad can I actually touch you? He said nothing but I reached out my hands and I actually touched him and I felt him and I knew that there was a life after death when I got up from the dream. Today, I am frequently dreaming to work out various issues.

Epilogue

"Understand me. I'm not like an ordinary world. I have my madness, I live in another dimension and I do not have time for things that have no soul."

~ Charles Bukowski

"I know this now: I am inevitable. I sincerely believe the only thing that can stop me now is insanity, disease, or death. The plays I am going to write may not be suited to the tender bellies of old maids, sweet young girls, or Baptist Ministers but they will be true and honest and courageous, and the rest doesn't matter… life, life, life, the only thing that matters. It is savage, cruel, kind, noble, passionate, selfish, generous, stupid, ugly, beautiful, painful, joyous it is all these, and more, and it's all these I want to know and, by God, I shall, though they crucify me for it. I will go to the ends of the earth to find it, to understand it … and I will put it on paper, and make it true and beautiful."

~ Thomas Wolfe's Letters to his Mother How we See …

"We don't see things as they are, we see them as we are." Anais Nn

I used to think I was the strangest person in the world but then I thought there are so many people in the world, there must be someone just like me who feels bizarre and flawed in the same ways I do. I would imagine her, and imagine that she must be out there thinking of me too. Well, I hope that if you are out there and read this and know that, yes, it's true I'm here, and I'm just as strange as you.

~ Frida Kahlo

Do stuff. Be clenched, curious. Not waiting for inspiration's shove or society's kiss on your forehead. Pay attention. It is all about paying attention. Attention is vitality. It connects you with others. It makes you eager. Stay eager.

~ Susan Sontag

"Safety is not the absence of threat. It is the presence of connection."
~ Gabor Mate

"You see what you think, you see what you feel, you are what you see if with the camera you can make others see it - that is photography."

~ Ernst Haas

"Beauty begins the moment you decide to be yourself."
~ Coco Chanel

At any given moment, you have the power to say: This is not how the story is going to end.

I think it's a deep consolation to know that spiders dream, that monkeys tease predators, that dolphins have accents, that lions can be scared silly by a lone mongoose, that otters hold hands, and ants bury their dead. That there isn't their life and our life. Nor your life and my life.

That it is just one teetering and endless thread and all of us, all of us, are entangled with it as deep as entanglement goes.

~ Kate Forster

Remedios Varo believed in magic. She had an animistic faith in the power of objects and in the interrelatedness of plant, animal, human, and mechanical worlds. The story is told that one evening on a Mexican street she found a plant being sold that produced fruits that looked like eggs. Fascinated, she brought one to her apartment, set it in the center of her plant-filled terrace in the moonlight and placed her tubes of paint around it. She felt that this special plant, her paints, and the moon were harmonious together and that their conjunction would proved auspicious for the next day of painting...Varo held a mystical belief in forces beyond the self, in powers beyond that of the individual that can influence and direct events.

~ Woman's Art Journal 1980

Beyond the WALL "For the inhabitants of the mental asylum, it is the "outside" that is abnormal."

~Vittorino Andreoli

There is a kind of sadness that comes from knowing too much, from seeing the world as it truly is. It is the sadness of understanding that life is not a grand adventure, but a series of small, insignificant moments, that love is not a fairy tale, but a fragile, fleeting emotion, that happiness is not a permanent state, but a rare, fleeting glimpse of something we can never hold onto. And in that understanding, there is a profound loneliness, a sense of being cut off from the world, from other people, from oneself.

~ Virginia Woolf

The tree of birth and death Forest Shiva

~ Forest Vishnu Flowing in Flowing out Endless cycle

The wheel of forest life
~ Tracy Hamby

Art is a wound turned into light.
~ Georges Braque

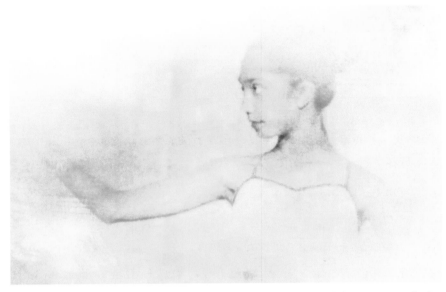

My work centers on memory, dreams & personal history coupled
with a loved of the deep elegance found in nature:

it's poetic form,

perfect symmetry,

color that speaks

and endless mystery.

Namaste